Broadcasting From Beyond

Tim Root

Contents

Dedication

To the 1981 DCA World Champions,
The Connecticut Hurricanes.

Acknowledgments

To my Mom and Dad and my friends that crossed over.

About the Author

Tim Root has spent more than five decades studying and interpreting the skies. A professional meteorologist for over fifty-two years, Tim has forecasted weather patterns across the United States for radio stations, newspapers, and media outlets. His dedication to understanding the atmosphere has taken him from local forecasts to international events.

He served as the meteorologist for the French team during the **America's Cup** in San Diego in the mid-1990s and later became the **official meteorologist for the America's Cup** itself in the late 1990s. Throughout his career, he has been trusted by countless broadcasters and organizations, providing accurate forecasts that have guided major sporting events and informed millions of viewers. He also worked as the **morning weather producer for CBS in San Diego, California**, where his early morning reports became a familiar voice to audiences across the region.

Alongside his lifelong work in meteorology, Tim has always been fascinated by the connection between the natural and spiritual worlds. His deep curiosity about the unseen and his personal encounters with the mysterious inspired his book *Broadcasting from Beyond*, a moving collection of true experiences that explore the moments when faith, love, and the spirit world meet.

Today, Tim continues to forecast the weather nationwide while living in **Lakeland, Florida**, where the skies and the soul seem to speak in harmony. His work and his writing share one guiding message, that love, faith, and connection never end, and that even beyond this life, the heart still finds a way to be heard.

Introduction

For more than half a century I have made my living studying the skies. I have read the signs of weather, watched storms take shape across the oceans, and told people when rain would come or when the sun would return. My name is **Tim Root**, and I have been a meteorologist for fifty-two years. I have forecasted the weather for radio stations across the country, for newspapers, and even for international sailing competitions. In the mid-nineties I served as a meteorologist for the French team during the **America's Cup** in San Diego, and later I became the official meteorologist for the event itself. I have worked for **CBS in San Diego, California**, producing morning weather broadcasts and helping millions of people plan their days.

Weather has always fascinated me because it connects heaven and earth. It is what we see when invisible forces move through the air, shaping clouds, forming winds, and creating patterns that no human hand can touch. What I never expected was that, outside my profession, I would one day witness another kind of invisible force, one not found in weather charts or radar screens. It was a force that could move through rooms, whisper in the dark, and reveal itself when I least expected it.

This book is not about weather forecasts or science. It is about the unseen world that exists beside us, the world of spirits, energies, and divine messages that most people never notice. Over the years, I have come to believe that life continues after death, that our loved ones do not disappear when their bodies fail, and that sometimes they find ways to let us know they are still near.

I am not a novelist, and this is not a work of imagination. Every story you will read in these pages is drawn directly from my own experience. They are the moments that have stayed with me long after they happened. Some took place when I was alone, others when I was with friends or family, but each one left a mark that changed how I see the world.

I began writing these events down because they refused to fade. Over time, I realized that I was being shown something. These encounters were not random. They were lessons, reminders that there is more to life than what we can measure or explain. I decided to share them because I believe they might bring comfort, curiosity, and even peace to others who have wondered about what lies beyond.

When people first hear about spirits or ghosts, they often think of horror movies or haunted houses. That is not what this is about. The experiences I share are not meant to frighten but to open the heart to possibility. Some are eerie, yes, and some left me shaken, but behind the mystery there is always warmth, always love.

Through the years I have come to understand that when the physical world grows quiet, another world becomes easier to hear. The silence between footsteps, the flicker of a light, the scent of something familiar when no one is near—all of these can be ways that spirits reach out. They are signs that the boundary between this life and the next is thinner than we think.

I grew up in **Bridgeport, Connecticut**, in a time when people did not speak much about the supernatural. My earliest memories are filled with weather events that inspired me to study the atmosphere, but even as a child, I sensed there was something else in the world, something unseen. That sense would grow stronger through the years, and as I moved from one state to another, it seemed to follow me.

In **California**, I began to experience the first undeniable signs. Voices in the night that had no earthly source, lights that turned on and off in response to my words, dreams that foretold real events, and strange photographs that revealed figures no one had seen. There were moments that could chill the blood, yet each one carried its own quiet message. I learned to listen carefully.

When I later moved to **Florida**, the encounters continued, but their nature changed. The fear gave way to something gentler, something deeply spiritual. After my mother passed away, I began to receive signs that she was still close—through butterflies, through scents, through coincidences so exact that they could not be accidents. These experiences brought me more comfort than I could ever describe.

The stories that follow are arranged in the order they happened, beginning with my years in California and ending with my time in Florida. Some of them are personal, others involve friends or family who had experiences of their own. All of them are true to the best of my knowledge. They are not exaggerated, and they have not been changed for dramatic effect. I want readers to feel what I felt, to imagine the air in the room, the sudden stillness, the soft voice that should not be there, and the awe that follows.

I am aware that some readers will approach these pages with skepticism. That is fine. I was a man of science before I ever believed in the paranormal. I still believe in evidence and observation. But sometimes evidence comes in forms that instruments cannot record. The experiences I describe are not things that could be tested in a lab, yet they happened. They are as real to me as the storms I tracked across the Atlantic.

You may wonder why someone with a scientific mind would write a book about spirits and signs from beyond. The answer is simple. Because I have lived through things that science cannot explain, and I cannot ignore them. When something invisible turns on a light at your request, when a dream warns you of an event that comes true, when a photograph captures a face that was not there a moment before, you begin to understand that the world is larger than any textbook can hold.

There is also another reason I wrote this book. I want to leave a record. I am not a young man anymore, and I have seen how easily memories can fade. These stories are part of who I am, part of the strange and beautiful path that has carried me through life. I want my family, my friends, and anyone who reads these words to know that I have felt the presence of something divine.

What I hope readers take away from these pages is not fear but faith. Faith that death is not an end, that love survives, and that those we have lost may still walk beside us in ways we cannot see. I hope that people who have felt unexplainable things—an object moving, a familiar scent filling a room, a sudden warmth during sorrow—will find comfort here and realize they are not alone.

You will notice that I speak of both ghosts and God in these pages. To me, they are not separate. The same power that shapes the weather and the tides also connects our souls. Whether we call it spirit, energy, or divine will, it moves between us and through us. The more I have accepted that truth, the more peace I have found.

I do not claim to be psychic, but I can channel spirits as at times messages have come through that no ordinary explanation can cover. I have used voice recorders, cameras, and intuition, each offering glimpses into that invisible world. Sometimes the messages were kind, other times they carried warnings, but always they reminded me that our world is not alone.

Every chapter in this book is built from a real event. Some are short, others stretch over days or weeks. Together they form a timeline of my encounters with what I believe to be the spirit world. You will read about the first voice I heard in the middle of the night, about lights that obeyed unseen hands, about photographs that captured faces from another time, and about signs from loved ones who had passed on. You will also hear about the faith that kept me grounded when fear tried to take over.

In sharing these stories, I do not ask anyone to abandon reason. I only ask that you read with an open mind and an open heart. If even one of these experiences helps someone believe that there is something beyond the grave, then I will have done what I set out to do.

For me, this is more than a book. It is a testimony, a record of the mysterious partnership between the physical and the spiritual. It is proof, in my own way that we are never truly alone.

So now, I invite you to join me as we travel through the events that shaped my life and my faith. From my early years in California, where the first strange signs began, to the quiet moments in Florida where I felt my mother's presence once again, every story is a piece of the same truth. The spirit world is real, it is near, and sometimes, if we listen closely, it speaks.

Chapter One

The Beginning of a

Weather Man's Journey

My life has always seemed to weave everything together. I was born in a year marked by hurricanes, later chose meteorology as my career, and even joined a drum and bugle corps named, of all things, The Hurricanes. The corps was founded in 1955, the very year I was born. Sometimes things really do fall into place.

I spent seven years with The Hurricanes, playing twenty-four-inch cymbals alongside more than a hundred team members. In 1981, after losing every show and finishing second or third all season, we traveled to Philadelphia for the Labor Day championships. Twenty-two thousand people watched the Connecticut Hurricanes become World Champions, defeating twenty other corps.

But that is not even the strangest part.

A week before the show, my gut told me to make a T-shirt with "Connecticut Hurricanes" on the front and on the back in big letters "And now we are the Nation's Best," lyrics from our corps song celebrating our 1967 and 1969 championship wins. We had lost almost every competition that year, so there was no reason to expect a miracle. But something told me to make the shirt anyway.

After we won, everyone asked, "Where did you get that shirt so fast, and how did you know?" At the time, I had no answer. But now I do. It was one more sign, one more message, that something in me was working beyond luck or coincidence. Something I had not yet learned to fully understand but could no longer ignore.

I marched one more year in 1982. We finished third, but my mind had already begun to open. Not just to the weather, but to the unseen, the unexplainable, and the quiet voice inside me that always seemed to know before I did.

Chapter Two
Voices in the Night

Location: El Cajon, California

Time: Early 1990s

The night was still, the kind of silence that wraps around a house after the city has gone to sleep. I had been living in my small apartment in El Cajon, California, for several months. My roommate was away visiting his family in Mexico, leaving me alone in the two-story home. It was a peaceful place by day, filled with sunlight and the sound of palm leaves brushing against the windows, but at night, the air felt different. There was a weight to it, something I could never quite explain.

That night I had fallen asleep earlier than usual. I had an early morning shift preparing weather reports for my clients on the radio. I remember turning off the bedside lamp and watching the faint orange glow from the streetlight outside flicker through the blinds. Everything was calm, perfectly ordinary, until around two in the morning.

That was when I heard it.

A voice, soft and clear, spoke into the darkness. "Hello."

I opened my eyes. My first thought was that it must have been someone outside, maybe a child from another apartment. I held my breath, listening. The voice came again, closer this time, almost beside my ear.

"Hello."

It was not a voice coming from the next apartment, nor a sound from outside. It came from the air around me, inside the room. The voice was young, like a boy's, polite yet curious. For a few seconds, I lay frozen, staring into the dim light that filtered through the blinds. My heart began to pound. I wanted to speak, but fear pinned me down.

After a moment the sound faded. The air was silent again, but my pulse was racing. I sat up and switched on the lamp, staring at the corners of the room. Nothing. The space was empty, yet I could still feel the presence of something unseen.

I told myself it might have been a dream, perhaps a sound from outside mixed into my half-conscious mind. It was easier to think that way. Eventually, I fell back asleep, though it was a restless sleep, filled with uneasy thoughts.

When morning came, the sun poured through the window as if to erase what had happened. I tried to shake off the feeling. I had a long day ahead. My routine was always the same: a shower, coffee, and then the steady rhythm of typing out my forecasts.

I stepped into the bathroom, turned on the water, and let the warm steam fill the room. The shower always cleared my head, but that morning felt different. The air was thick, and the quiet hum of the pipes seemed louder than usual. I brushed the thought away, finished up, and went to get dressed.

As I reached for my shirt, a sharp click broke the silence. I turned toward the sound. The light in my bedroom had switched on by itself.

I froze. The switch was across the room. My hand had not touched it.

The bulb glowed brightly, washing the room in a pale light. My first instinct was to laugh it off, to assume a faulty wire or loose connection. But something in my gut told me this was not a malfunction. I could feel it, a presence lingering in the air, faint but undeniable.

I decided to test it.

Speaking aloud felt strange, but I cleared my throat and said softly, "If someone is here, could you please turn the light off?"

For a few seconds, nothing happened. Then, without a sound, the light went out.

My breath caught in my throat. The room was once again dim, lit only by the sunlight filtering through the blinds. My heart was beating so hard I could hear it. I stood perfectly still, afraid to move.

Then I whispered, "Can you turn it back on?"

The switch clicked again, and the light returned.

I do not know how long I stood there, staring. The logical part of my mind fought with what I had just seen. I had been trained to look for explanations, to observe patterns, to believe in data and evidence. But this defied all logic. The light was not flickering randomly, it was responding.

I asked one last time, "Please, turn the light off."

And it did.

The bulb dimmed and went dark. The silence that followed was so heavy it felt alive. I could feel my hands trembling, not just from fear but from awe. I whispered a quiet "thank you" without even knowing why.

That was my first undeniable experience with what I would later call the other side. At the time, I did not yet understand what it meant. All I knew was that something, or someone, had answered me.

***

In the days that followed, I could not stop thinking about it. The memory replayed again and again in my mind, the click of the switch, the perfect timing, the sense of a quiet intelligence watching from just beyond sight. I told no one at first. Who would believe me? I was a meteorologist, a man of logic and observation, not superstition. Yet, deep down, I knew what I had felt.

A few days later, I decided to speak aloud in my room again, just to see if it would happen. I waited until the evening when the house was still. I sat on the edge of my bed and said softly, "If you're here, can you give me a sign?"

This time, nothing happened. No voice, no click, only the distant hum of the refrigerator. I began to wonder if that first encounter had been a one-time event. Still, I could not shake the feeling that I had opened a door.

Over the following weeks, I noticed small things, objects slightly moved, faint tapping on the walls, a light flickering at odd moments. They were subtle, easy to dismiss, but I had started paying attention. The house did not feel empty anymore. It felt as though it was listening.

One evening, I called a friend who had always been interested in the paranormal. When I told him what had happened, he said, "Tim, maybe it's a child spirit. They sometimes attach to kind people." His words stayed with me. I remembered the voice, it did sound young, like a boy saying hello for the first time.

From then on, I began to speak to the spirit gently whenever I felt its presence. I never used harsh words or demanded proof. I simply spoke as if to a guest. Sometimes I would say, "If you're around, I hope you're at peace." Other times, I just thanked it for being kind. I never felt danger from it, only curiosity.

Months passed, and though the voice never returned as clearly as that first night, the memory of it remained one of the most powerful experiences of my life. It opened my mind to something beyond my understanding. It was the first time I truly accepted that there are forces in this world that science cannot explain.

15

That encounter also changed how I looked at my work. As a meteorologist, I had always focused on patterns, the way air moves, how pressure changes, how energy transfers. I started to wonder if the spirit world worked in a similar way. Maybe spirits, too, were forms of energy moving through unseen currents. Maybe their voices were just another kind of wave, not unlike the frequencies I used for radio transmissions.

I began to see connections everywhere. When the wind rattled the windowpanes, I thought of voices carried on air. When lightning split the sky, I imagined unseen powers reminding us of what lies beyond.

Over time, I told a few close friends about what had happened. Some listened with fascination, others smiled politely but said nothing. I did not blame them. It is one thing to believe in ghosts when you hear someone else's story, and another to believe when you are the one lying awake in a dark room while the lights turn themselves on and off.

To this day, I can still remember the tone of that young voice, clear and almost friendly. It never said more than a greeting, never tried to frighten me. It was as if it just wanted to be noticed, to be heard. That simple word, "Hello," has stayed with me all these years.

If that first encounter had not happened, I might have dismissed later events as coincidence. But after that night, I began to watch for signs everywhere. It was the beginning of a journey that would take me far beyond what I ever expected to see.

That night in California marked the first chapter of a much larger story, a story that would follow me through different homes, different states, and different stages of life. It was the start of my understanding that life and death are not as separate as we think. The boundaries are thin, and sometimes, if the air is still enough, voices can pass through.

As I would learn in the years to come, that "hello" was not just a greeting. It was an invitation.

Chapter Three
The Spirit in the House

Location: El Cajon, California

Time: Mid-1990s

The years I spent in El Cajon were some of the most unusual of my life. It was a quiet suburb on the eastern edge of San Diego County, where the desert heat softened into cool coastal nights. By that time, I had already been working for radio stations across the country, preparing weather reports every morning before dawn. My days followed a rhythm of forecasts, charts, and calls from producers, but when the sun went down, my world became very different.

I shared the house with a roommate who came from a family in Baja, Mexico. They were known for their long-standing connection to spiritual practices that most people would call witchcraft. He would sometimes tell stories of his grandmother, a woman who healed with herbs and whispered to the wind. I had always taken those stories lightly, thinking of them as old folk tales meant to entertain. I had no idea how deeply those beliefs would come to shape what happened inside that house.

The building itself was ordinary enough, a two-story place with white stucco walls and a narrow staircase that creaked under every step. The living room opened into a small kitchen, and upstairs were two bedrooms that looked out over the street. From the outside, it appeared peaceful. Yet from the first week I moved in, I could sense that something about it felt unsettled, as if the air itself carried memories.

At first, I brushed off the oddities. A flickering light. A song that played faintly from the stereo even though it was turned off. A door that would open slightly, then close again without a breeze. My roommate laughed when I mentioned it. "The house likes attention," he said. I thought he was joking.

One night in late summer, he was downstairs watching television while I was in my bedroom reviewing the next day's forecasts. I remember the sound of the crickets outside and the faint hum of the refrigerator. The temperature was warm, but suddenly a cold current passed through the room, strong enough to raise the hairs on my arms. Before I could move, the bedroom light flickered three times and went out.

I called down to my roommate. "Did the power go out?"

"No," he answered. "Everything's fine down here."

I tried the switch again, and the light came back on. The moment it did, I caught a faint whisper, a voice so soft I almost thought it was the wind. I could not make out the words, only that they came from somewhere behind me.

That was the first time I felt truly uneasy.

The days that followed were filled with strange happenings. The hallway light would turn on and off without anyone touching it. The radio would come alive in the middle of the night, playing soft static instead of music. I began to lose sleep. I told myself that electrical issues might be to blame, but deep down, I knew there was more.

My roommate seemed amused by it all. He would walk around the house with a smirk, sometimes speaking softly in Spanish as if addressing someone invisible. When I asked him what he was saying, he shrugged. "Just saying hello to the ones who live here," he said.

That statement chilled me. The ones who live here.

I wanted to believe he was teasing, but every day brought something new. A cup sliding an inch across the table. Footsteps overhead when both of us were downstairs. Music playing faintly from the stereo even when the power cord was unplugged.

Then came the night I will never forget.

It was near midnight. I had gone to bed early because I needed to wake around 2am to record my weather segments. The house was quiet except for the steady ticking of the clock in the hallway. I had just started to drift off when I heard heavy footsteps on the wooden floor downstairs. At first, I assumed my roommate was still awake, but the steps grew louder, climbing the staircase one by one.

The sound stopped outside my bedroom door. I waited for a knock, but none came.

Then, slowly, the doorknob turned.

The door opened only an inch before freezing in place. The hallway light was on, and I could see the faint outline of the doorknob glinting. The light over the dining room table came crushing down and broke.

I looked over to my bedroom across the hall, and for a second or two I saw the old man who had died in the house coming toward me very quickly. He passed straight through me like a cold breeze and then went out the window one afternoon. I will remember that for the rest of my life.

My body refused to move. Every muscle locked in place. My mind screamed at me to call out, but my voice would not come.

The air grew heavy, pressing down on me like a weight. I could hear my heartbeat echoing in my ears. For several endless seconds, I lay there, eyes wide open, unable to move or speak. It felt as if something unseen was holding me still, testing me, observing me.

Then, just as suddenly as it had started, the pressure lifted. I gasped for breath and sat up, drenched in sweat. I forced my voice to work and shouted for my roommate.

He came running upstairs. "What happened?" he asked.

"There was someone at the door," I said. "I heard footsteps. The doorknob turned."

We checked the hallway. Nothing. Every window was locked, the alarm light still green. He frowned but did not seem surprised.

"It is just them again," he said quietly.

I wanted to argue, to tell him that this was no joke, but his calm expression stopped me. I realized that, to him, this was normal.

After that night, the activity grew stronger. Sometimes I would wake to faint music drifting through the house, as though a distant radio were playing an old tune. At other times, the lights would blink in rhythm, as if responding to unseen voices. I began to keep a small flashlight on the nightstand, though I rarely used it.

On New Year's Eve that year, my roommate had gone back to Mexico to visit his family again, leaving me alone in the house. I decided to stay in, cook myself a small dinner, and watch the festivities on television. As the clock neared midnight, I stood in the kitchen stirring a pot of pasta when I heard laughter coming from upstairs.

It sounded like a group of people, faint but cheerful, raising glasses in a toast. I froze with the spoon still in my hand. The laughter continued, followed by the clinking of glass against glass, as though an invisible celebration were taking place in the bedroom above.

Every window in the house was closed. The night outside was cold and quiet.

I turned off the stove and started up the stairs, each step creaking beneath my feet. The moment I reached the landing, the sounds stopped. The silence that followed was almost physical. I searched the rooms. Empty. No one there.

I stood in the doorway of my bedroom for several minutes, listening. Nothing. But the air carried a faint scent of perfume, old-fashioned and floral, like something from another era. I whispered softly, "Happy New Year," then returned downstairs.

That was the night I realized something had truly changed. The house was no longer just a home. It had become a place where the worlds overlapped. I no longer felt angry or frightened, only aware. There was life on both sides of the wall.

After that, I tried to make peace with whatever shared that space with me. I began leaving a small lamp on in the hallway and speaking kindly whenever I felt the air grow colder. "You are welcome here as long as you mean no harm," I would say. It seemed to help. The lights flickered less often, and the footsteps became fewer.

When my roommate returned from Mexico, I told him everything. He nodded slowly. "Sometimes the door opens wider than we expect," he said.

His words stayed with me.

Even now, when I look back on those months in El Cajon, I can still remember the feeling of the floorboards under my feet, the faint hum of the appliances, and the sense that eyes were watching from just beyond sight. It was not an evil presence, though it could be overwhelming. It was curious, restless, and at times almost playful.

That house taught me that the veil between this world and the next is thin. It can be brushed aside by emotion, by memory, or by the simple act of attention. I believe my roommate's family history, steeped in rituals and old beliefs, might have opened that doorway, but I also believe I was meant to witness it.

Those nights in California became the foundation for everything that followed. They prepared me for the experiences I would later have in Florida, where the spirits felt closer, warmer, and filled with love instead of mystery.

When people ask whether I ever feared for my safety, I tell them no. What I felt was not danger but discovery. Once you realize that the world is bigger than what you can touch, fear turns into awe.

El Cajon was where I learned that the unseen is always near. Sometimes it walks beside us on creaking stairs, sometimes it laughs above us on a quiet New Year's Eve, and sometimes it simply waits for us to notice.

That house, with all its strange sounds and shifting lights, was not haunted by the dead. It was alive with memory, a place where spirits paused long enough to remind me that they were still here.

And from that moment forward, I never doubted again.

Chapter Four
The New Year's Visitors

Location: El Cajon, California

Time: New Year's Eve, Late 1990s

The end of that year came quietly. The calendar was turning once again, and the house in El Cajon had settled into an uneasy calm. My roommate had returned to Mexico for the holidays to spend time with his family, leaving me alone for several weeks. I did not mind the solitude. After months of strange occurrences, I thought a little peace and quiet would do me good.

I kept my schedule as usual, preparing early morning forecasts and sending updates to radio stations across the country. The winter weather in California was mild that year, just a faint chill in the evenings and a few rainy days. But as New Year's Eve approached, I noticed something familiar

27

returning to the air. A heaviness. It felt like a memory pressing against the walls.

That afternoon I went about my chores as normal. The sun was low, the sky brushed with the soft orange of early evening. I had decided to stay home that night, away from the noise of the celebrations. I had no desire to be out among crowds. Instead, I planned a quiet evening with a home-cooked meal, some soft music, and the television coverage of New Year's festivities across the country.

Around seven o'clock I began to prepare dinner. I filled a pot with water, chopped vegetables, and let the familiar rhythm of cooking settle my thoughts. The kitchen was small but cozy, with a window overlooking the backyard. I could see the faint outline of trees swaying in the wind, their branches catching the last traces of daylight.

As I stirred the pot, a wave of nostalgia washed over me. I thought of my family back in Connecticut, of how New Year's had once meant gatherings filled with laughter and noise. It had been years since I had celebrated it that way. Now, my only company was the soft hum of the refrigerator and the rhythmic tapping of my spoon against the pan.

At around nine, I sat down to eat. The night was still. The neighborhood seemed unusually quiet for a holiday. I finished my meal, washed the dishes, and settled into the living room to watch television. On the screen, the countdown festivities from New York lit up the night with color and sound. I watched the crowd cheer, watched the ball drop in Times Square, and listened to the laughter of strangers on the other side of the country.

It was comforting and lonely all at once.

When the broadcast ended, I turned off the television. The house fell silent again, except for the faint ticking of the wall clock. I decided to head to the kitchen to make some tea before going to bed.

That was when I heard it.

From upstairs came the sound of voices.

At first, I thought the neighbors were having a party. But the voices were not muffled through walls or ceilings. They were inside the house.

I stopped where I stood, the teacup still in my hand. The sound grew clearer. It was not loud, but it carried the unmistakable warmth of conversation, of people gathered together in celebration. I could hear laughter, soft and cheerful. Then came the faint, unmistakable clinking of glass, the sound of a toast.

My heart began to beat faster.

I set the cup down on the counter and listened carefully. The sounds were coming from directly above me, from my own bedroom.

The first thought that crossed my mind was that an intruder had broken in. The second, which came quickly after, was that this felt far too familiar. The air was heavy again, the same electric stillness that had filled the house during earlier encounters.

I took a deep breath and whispered to myself, "Stay calm."

I stepped into the hallway and began climbing the stairs. Each step creaked softly under my weight. The higher I went, the clearer the sounds became. The voices were mixed, men and women, laughing, talking, their tones warm and friendly. I heard the soft hum of what might have been music, faint, old-fashioned, like something from another time.

When I reached the landing, I paused. The door to my bedroom was closed, but light glowed faintly from the gap beneath it. My hand trembled slightly as I reached for the doorknob. I turned it slowly and pushed the door open.

Silence.

The room was empty.

The light that I thought I had seen was gone. The air was still, colder than before. I stepped inside, my eyes scanning every corner. The bed was neatly made, the curtains drawn, the lamp untouched. Everything was exactly as I had left it.

Yet the scent of the room had changed.

It smelled faintly of perfume, old and sweet, the kind that lingered in the air long after someone left. It reminded me of the sort of fragrance my mother used to wear when I was a child. It was impossible for it to be there, no one had been in that room but me for days.

I stood there for a long time, listening. The voices were gone, but the silence was not empty. It felt filled, as if someone invisible was still present, watching quietly.

After several minutes, I whispered, "Happy New Year."

I do not know why I said it, only that it felt right.

The air in the room seemed to move then, a faint shift, as if a breeze had passed through even though the windows were closed. Then everything was still again.

I returned downstairs and sat on the couch. The ticking of the clock sounded louder than before. I checked the time, twelve fifteen. The New Year had already arrived.

I stared at the blank television screen and thought about what had just happened. There had been laughter, glasses clinking, music, and a sense of joy. None of it felt threatening. It was as though a celebration was taking place in another dimension, one that brushed against mine for just a few moments.

Later that night, as I tried to fall asleep, I replayed every sound in my mind. The laughter had been so clear, so human, that part of me almost expected to hear it again. But the house remained quiet.

When morning came, sunlight streamed through the windows as if nothing unusual had occurred. Still, the air carried a strange lightness, as though whatever had visited the night before had left a trace of happiness behind.

I brewed my morning coffee and sat at the kitchen table thinking about what had happened. It was not the first time I had heard unexplained sounds in that house, but this one was different. It was not frightening. It was festive. It felt as though spirits had come together to mark the passing of another year, just as we do.

Perhaps they had been residents long before me. Perhaps they were visitors from another realm, drawn to the energy of celebration. Or perhaps, in some way I cannot explain, they were echoes of time itself, moments replaying endlessly in a place that remembers.

The scientist in me still tried to find logic in it. Could it have been sound from outside, traveling through vents or walls? Could a neighbor's gathering have carried upward and distorted the direction? But no matter how I analyzed it, the facts did not fit. The voices had come from my room. The laughter had been right above my head.

That experience taught me something important. Not all encounters with the spirit world are rooted in fear. Sometimes, they carry warmth, as if those who have passed still find joy in the traditions they once loved.

In the days that followed, I spoke to my roommate by phone. I told him what had happened. He listened quietly and then said, "Maybe they were celebrating with you."

His calmness no longer surprised me. He had always spoken of the house as if it were alive, as if it held company beyond what the eye could see.

That New Year's Eve marked the first time I began to think of the spirits not as intruders, but as neighbors, inhabitants of a parallel world that sometimes overlaps with ours. They seemed harmless, even cheerful. Their energy did not drain or frighten me, it uplifted me.

In the evenings that followed, I often sat in the living room reading or preparing my next day's forecasts. Every so often, I thought I heard faint movement upstairs, the creak of a step, a soft rustle, and I would smile rather than tense.

The house no longer felt haunted. It felt shared.

I began leaving a small nightlight on at the foot of the stairs. It was not out of fear but out of respect. A gesture of peace for whatever unseen company might wander through those rooms when midnight came.

Months later, when I finally moved from that house, I stood for a while in the doorway, looking back at the empty rooms. I could almost imagine the laughter echoing faintly through the air once more, the soft ring of glass, and the warmth that had filled that New Year's night.

I said goodbye out loud, my voice gentle. "Thank you for letting me stay."

The air seemed to stir one last time, a whisper of acknowledgment, and then the house grew still.

When I left that house, I thought I was leaving the supernatural behind. But as I would soon discover, spirits do not always stay in one place. Some follow quietly, drawn not by buildings or land, but by the hearts that recognize them.

And when I arrived in Florida, I found that the story was far from over.

Chapter Five
The Move Eastward

Location: From El Cajon, California to Lakeland, Florida

Time: Late 1990s to Early 2000s

Leaving California was not an easy decision. The state had been my home for decades, the place where I had built my career, made friends, and seen more wonders of weather than I could count. I had forecasted storms rolling in from the Pacific, reported droughts, and watched the beauty of the coastline change with the seasons. But after everything that had happened, the footsteps, the laughter, the lights that moved without touch, and the image of Jesus that appeared on my cymbal, I began to feel that California had given me all the signs it was meant to give.

It was time for a new beginning.

I wanted a slower pace, a quieter life, a place where I could work, reflect, and perhaps understand what all those experiences had meant. I did not feel chased away. It was more like being gently guided to move on, as if unseen hands were steering me toward another chapter.

I chose Florida.

The decision came naturally. I had contacts there through my work with radio stations, and the climate was familiar to me, full of weather patterns that had always fascinated me, hurricanes, warm fronts, humid air masses that seemed alive. But deep down, I think I was drawn there for another reason. I did not know it then, but Florida would become the setting for a series of experiences that would bring me closer to faith and to understanding than ever before.

When I began packing my things, I found myself pausing often, looking around the house that had held so many strange and powerful moments. Every corner seemed to have a memory attached to it. The hallway where I had heard voices. The stairs that had creaked under invisible feet. The kitchen that had filled with laughter one New Year's Eve when no one else was home. And of course, the bedroom where the cymbal lay still carrying the image that refused to fade.

I wrapped the cymbals carefully and placed them in the case, whispering a short prayer. "Thank you," I said quietly, unsure whether I was speaking to the object or to something listening through it.

As I loaded the moving truck, the California sun was bright, but the air carried a coolness that hinted at farewell. I stood in the driveway one last time, looking back at the house. The white stucco walls glowed in the morning light, and for a brief moment, I thought I saw a faint flicker from the upstairs window, like someone turning on the light to say goodbye. Then it was gone.

The road east stretched out before me, thousands of miles of changing landscapes. I drove through deserts, across mountains, and along highways that cut through endless plains. Each state felt different, each sky a new canvas. At night, when I stopped at small motels, I sometimes felt that same quiet presence settle near me. It was never heavy, never frightening, just familiar, as though a gentle reminder that I was not traveling alone.

Some nights, while looking out at the stars, I wondered if the spirit world followed people across distances. Could a presence that once spoke to you in a California bedroom find you again under a Florida sky? I did not know, but part of me hoped so.

The drive took several days. The closer I got to the South, the more the scenery changed. The air grew warmer, thicker with moisture, and the trees became taller, their branches draped with moss that swayed like quiet ghosts in the wind. When I finally crossed into Florida, I rolled down the window and breathed in the heavy, sweet air. It smelled of rain and earth and new beginnings.

I settled in a small city called Lakeland, situated between Tampa and Orlando. The name itself felt like a promise of peace. My new home was modest, a single-story house surrounded by trees and open sky. The moment I stepped inside, I could feel the difference. The air was still, but not heavy. It felt welcoming. There was warmth in the light that filtered through the windows.

After unpacking, I took a walk through the neighborhood. The streets were quiet, lined with gardens and old oak trees. A few neighbors waved as I passed, friendly but not intrusive. I noticed the song of insects rising and falling like a constant heartbeat in the background. It was a sound I would come to love.

At night, the Florida air was alive. Crickets, frogs, and the soft hum of distant traffic filled the darkness. I began to sleep better than I had in years. It was as if the move had lifted a weight from me.

Still, I could not forget California. The image of Jesus on the cymbal stayed vivid in my mind. I kept the case stored in the corner of my new bedroom, unopened, yet always near. Sometimes I would glance at it before turning off the light, wondering if it might glow faintly in the dark.

My mother had passed away not long before I moved, and her memory was a constant companion. I often thought of her when I felt alone. She had always encouraged me to trust both my intuition and my faith, to see the world not only as a scientist but as a believer. In quiet moments, I could almost hear her voice saying, "Keep your heart open, Tim. The world is bigger than what you can measure."

It was that advice that stayed with me as I began to rebuild my life in Florida.

My work continued much as before. I provided forecasts for radio stations across the country, often starting before dawn. My days were filled with data and communication, but my evenings belonged to reflection. I started keeping a journal again, recording my thoughts, dreams, and the small coincidences that felt too meaningful to ignore.

One of the first things I noticed after settling in was how connected Florida felt to the elements. The sky changed quickly here, shifting from sunlight to thunder in minutes. Clouds would gather on the horizon, build into towers of gray, then release rain so heavy it seemed to cleanse everything in sight. After each storm, the air shimmered with life, as though the world itself had been renewed.

It was in that environment, surrounded by the unpredictable beauty of weather and the quiet comfort of solitude, that new experiences began to unfold. They were different from what I had known in California. There were no footsteps or flickering lights at first, only subtle moments that carried meaning, a butterfly landing near me, the sudden scent of something familiar, the feeling of a gentle presence close by.

I did not realize it then, but those small signs were the beginning of a new chapter, one filled with messages of peace and reassurance rather than mystery and fear.

Looking back, I understand now that the move to Florida was not random. I was being led there. California had taught me to believe. Florida would teach me to trust.

Before I closed the California chapter of my life completely, I made a quiet promise to myself. I would not run from what I did not understand. Instead, I would document it, respect it, and share it, because maybe these experiences were not meant for me alone. Maybe they were meant to remind others that there is something beyond what we can see.

That thought gave me courage.

In the months after my move, as the last boxes were unpacked and my new routines took shape, I felt something shift inside me. The fear that had once followed me during the nights in El Cajon was replaced by calm. I began to see the spiritual world not as a separate place but as something intertwined with our own, like two melodies playing together in harmony.

There were moments when I would sit outside on the porch after a storm and watch the sunset turn the clouds pink and gold. The air would still, and for a moment, everything would fall silent. In that silence, I often felt the same comforting awareness that had first spoken to me years ago through a flickering light and a soft voice in the dark.

It had followed me, not to haunt me, but to guide me.

I understood then that the journey from California to Florida was not only a move across states. It was a passage of faith, from uncertainty to understanding, from fear to peace.

That realization marked the true beginning of my Florida years. And as I would soon discover, the spirits had followed, not with mischief or warning, but with love.

The first sign came quietly, carried on wings of color, in the shape of a butterfly.

Chapter Six
The Salem Trip

Location: Salem, Massachusetts

Time: Early 2000's

I felt the need for a change of scenery. My work as a meteorologist kept me busy, but my mind was often caught between the charts and the memories of that strange house where I had lived. I still heard noises sometimes, even when I was away from home, faint echoes that reminded me of footsteps or whispers. I began to wonder if the presence that had revealed itself to me had followed along, or if I had simply become more aware of what had always been around.

It was during that period that my friend, the same roommate who had lived with me in Lakeland, suggested we take a short trip to Boston. He wanted to visit his relatives in the area, and I had long been fascinated by history, especially anything tied to the unseen. When he mentioned that we could also spend a day in Salem, Massachusetts, something inside me immediately said yes. Salem had always been a place of mystery in American folklore, known for the witch trials of the 1600s and the energy that still seemed to linger there.

We packed our bags and flew out one chilly morning in late autumn. The flight from Florida to the East Coast took most of the day. By the time we arrived in Boston, the sky was the color of pewter. Low clouds hung over the harbor, and a fine drizzle coated the streets. It felt as if the entire city had been dipped in fog. To me, it was perfect.

We stayed the night at a small hotel near the city center. My friend, who came from a family of witches in Baja, Mexico, seemed energized by the idea of visiting Salem. He spoke of it with excitement, almost reverence. I could tell he felt a kind of connection to the place even before we arrived.

The next morning, we rented a car and drove the thirty miles north to Salem. The road wound past stretches of forest where the trees were bare and twisted, their branches reaching toward the sky like hands frozen in mid-gesture. A faint mist clung to the ground, and every now and then we passed through small towns that looked as though they had not changed in centuries.

When we reached Salem, the rain had turned to a steady drizzle. The streets were narrow and cobblestoned, lined with old houses that leaned slightly with age. We walked together through the town, stopping by antique shops and old inns. Everywhere there were reminders of what the town was known for. Signs read "Witch Tours," "Haunted Museum," and "Psychic Readings." To most visitors, it was all entertainment. To me, it felt different. There was something heavy in the air, a stillness that pressed against the chest. It was as if the town remembered.

Our first stop was an old cemetery near the heart of town. The gate creaked as we pushed it open, and inside, rows of gravestones stood crooked from years of frost and rain. Some dated back to the late 1600s. The ground was soft and uneven underfoot. We walked slowly, reading the names that time had almost erased.

I took out my digital camera. Photography had always been a hobby, and I wanted to capture the texture of the stones, the moss that had grown over the names, the way the gray sky reflected off the wet marble. I snapped a photo of my friend standing near one of the older graves. The picture appeared clear on the camera screen. Then I took another.

This time, a white mist drifted across the image. It was not in the air around us, only in the photo. I frowned and looked up. The air was still. I checked the lens for moisture, but it was dry. I took another shot of the same spot. The mist was gone.

"Look at this," I said, showing my friend the image.

He smiled, unfazed. "A spirit," he said simply.

His calmness made me uneasy. I looked back at the headstone. The name was barely legible, the letters carved so long ago they had softened into the stone. Something about it made me shiver. I took a few more photos, each one from a different angle. In one, there was nothing unusual. In another, the faint outline of a shape appeared behind my friend, like a face half formed from smoke.

We left the cemetery and continued walking through the old part of town. The rain began to fall harder, a thin coat soaked through my jacket. We found an old building marked as one of the historic witch houses and stopped to take a few pictures there as well. The structure leaned slightly forward, its dark windows reflecting the gray light of the afternoon.

As I raised the camera, I felt that same pressure in the air that I had felt back in Florida, a sense of being watched, not by one thing but by many. I took the picture.

When I looked at the screen, two faces appeared in the second floor window.

They were faint but clear enough to see. They looked human, but not quite. The expressions were blank, the eyes fixed forward. The first was a man, his features long and pale, and beside him another face, darker and harder to define. Neither had been visible when I looked through the viewfinder.

I stared at the image for several seconds before showing it to my friend.

"What do you think?" I asked.

He looked at the screen and nodded. "They are watching," he said softly. "Maybe they never left."

We stood there in the rain, both quiet. The town around us went about its business. Cars passed, and people hurried along the sidewalks under umbrellas, but I felt separated from it all. The photograph in my hand was proof that something beyond ordinary sight was still lingering in Salem.

That night we returned to Boston, but I could not stop looking at the pictures. In one, the mist seemed to curl around my friend's shoulders like a hand. In another, the faces in the window appeared sharper each time I zoomed in. There was even a faint glow around the edges, as if the light itself had shifted to reveal them.

I did not sleep much. Each time I closed my eyes, I saw those faces staring back. Not angry, not kind, simply aware.

The next morning, as we packed to return to Florida, my friend said something that stayed with me. "You see, Tim. The past is never gone. It only waits for someone to notice it again."

When I returned home to Lakeland, I printed the photos. Holding them in my hands made them feel more real, more tangible. I studied them under different lights, trying to find a rational explanation. Perhaps a trick of reflection, or moisture in the air, or the peculiar way the camera sensor captured fog. But the more I looked, the less certain I became.

The faces did not behave like fog. They had form and proportion. They had intent. I could see the suggestion of eyes, the line of a nose, the faint outline of a mouth. It was not random.

For weeks, those images haunted me. Not in a fearful way, but as a reminder that I had witnessed something that few people ever do. Salem had opened another door. It was not just history that lived there. It was energy, memory, and presence. The town had seen too much sorrow to be silent.

I later read that many visitors to Salem reported similar experiences. Some claimed to see shadows move across the old houses. Others felt sudden cold spots while standing near the memorial stones. A few said they heard whispers carried by the wind. Whether or not all those stories were true, I knew what I had seen.

That trip changed the way I thought about spirits. Until then, I believed hauntings were tied only to people, to souls that lingered near those they loved. But Salem taught me that places themselves can remember. The walls, the ground, the air. They hold on to the emotions left behind. Pain, fear, injustice, and hope, all woven together into something that time cannot erase.

I still keep those photographs. They remind me of the day I stood in the rain with my friend, listening to the echo of the past through the lens of a camera. I no longer question whether spirits exist. I know they do. I have seen them, not just in dark rooms or quiet nights, but in the daylight, standing at the windows of history, waiting to be seen again.

Salem was a turning point for me. It was where I learned that not all spirits are connected to our own stories. Some belong to the land, to the events that shaped it. They are the silent witnesses, still watching, still waiting for someone to listen.

And on that cold, rainy afternoon in Massachusetts, I believe they found someone who did.

Chapter Seven

The Butterfly in the Garden

Location: Lakeland, Florida

Time: Early 2000s

The Florida sun has a way of wrapping itself around you. It is not just heat; it is presence. It hums in the air, glows through the trees, and touches everything it finds. When I first settled in Lakeland, I found comfort in that warmth. After the long drive from California, the open skies and green spaces made me feel lighter, as if life itself had pressed a reset button.

My house was small but peaceful. It sat on a quiet street lined with palm trees and the soft shadows of oaks. I had a little garden behind the house where I planted tomatoes, herbs, and a few flowers. Gardening became a routine for me. After years of constant deadlines and early mornings filled with weather reports, it felt good to have something living grow at its own pace under my care.

That garden would soon become the setting for one of the most meaningful experiences of my life.

It had been a few months since I moved to Florida. The weather was warm, and the air smelled of soil and citrus. My mother had passed away not long before I left California, and her memory stayed with me everywhere I went. I missed her deeply. She had always been the voice that grounded me, the one who reminded me to keep faith even when logic failed. I often thought about her when I was outside tending the plants.

One morning, I went out to pick some tomatoes. The vines had grown heavy with fruit, and the soil was still damp from the rain the night before. As I bent down to inspect a cluster of ripening tomatoes, something bright caught my eye.

A butterfly.

It was hovering just above the plants, its wings a vivid mix of orange, yellow, and black. It circled me once, twice, and then landed on the edge of a leaf right beside my hand.

At first, I just smiled. Florida was full of butterflies, after all. But as I watched it, I noticed it was not behaving like a normal butterfly. It did not flit away when I moved. It stayed close, almost as if it were studying me. Its wings opened and closed slowly, rhythmically, catching the sunlight like stained glass.

Something stirred in me then, something familiar.

I whispered, "Mom?"

The butterfly lifted into the air, circled me again, and then came to rest on my shoulder.

A wave of warmth spread through me. I cannot explain it, but in that moment, I felt as though she were there. The same calm presence I had felt in my old home during the moments of unexplainable peace returned, stronger than ever. My mother had always loved flowers and gardening. I remembered how she used to hum softly when she worked in her own garden, the way she would gently brush dirt from her hands and smile. The butterfly sat quietly on my shoulder for several seconds before it fluttered away toward the fence, vanishing into the sunlight.

I stood there for a long time, staring at the spot where it had disappeared. Something about the experience felt deliberate, like a message. I had seen signs before, but this one was different. It carried love.

Later that afternoon, as I was sitting inside drinking coffee, the calm was broken by the sudden sound of a car alarm blaring from the garage. I jumped up, startled. The alarm had never gone off before. My car was locked, and I had not touched the remote. I ran outside, pressed the button on the key fob, and the sound stopped.

The timing was too exact to ignore.

The butterfly, the warmth, the sense of her presence, and then the alarm — it was as if she was trying to get my attention. I whispered again, "Mom, are you here?"

A light breeze stirred the trees, rustling the leaves, and then silence. But that silence was full. It hummed softly, like an answer.

I knew in my heart it was her.

Later, when I spoke to a psychic who lived nearly a thousand miles away, she asked me a question that sent chills down my spine.

"Did you see a butterfly around you in the garden a few weeks ago?"

I remember the moment vividly. I was sitting at my desk, the phone pressed to my ear, staring out the window. My breath caught as I said, "Yes, I did."

She continued, "It was your mother. She came to let you know she is with you."

For a few seconds, I could not speak. The psychic could not possibly have known that. I had told no one. The experience had been so personal, so quiet, that I had kept it to myself.

Tears filled my eyes as she spoke. "Your mother wants you to know that she is happy where she is, and that you should not worry. She still watches over you."

I had to sit down. The confirmation was overwhelming.

I hung up the phone and looked out the window again, half expecting to see the butterfly waiting for me. The air outside shimmered in the heat, and though I saw no wings this time, I could feel the same peace.

From that day on, butterflies became a symbol of my mother's love. Whenever one appeared — whether in my garden, fluttering across the road while I was driving, or resting on a window — I took it as her way of saying hello. It was never random. The moments were always meaningful, arriving exactly when I needed them most.

One afternoon, a few weeks later, I was feeling low. Work had been stressful, and I was struggling to stay motivated. I sat on the back porch, staring out at the yard, lost in thought. Just then, a butterfly appeared again. This one was white, delicate, and luminous in the afternoon sun. It hovered for a moment, then drifted toward me, landing gently on the arm of my chair. I laughed softly, the heaviness in my chest lifting.

"All right, Mom," I whispered. "Message received."

The butterfly opened its wings, held them still for a second, and then flew away toward the trees.

Moments like that began to teach me that love does not end when a heartbeat stops. It changes form, but it continues, finding ways to reach across the boundaries that separate the physical and the spiritual.

Florida, I realized, had not only given me peace. It had given me a way to feel connected to her again. The strange energy that had once frightened me in California was now replaced by something gentle and pure. There were no footsteps, no voices in the dark. There were signs, yes, but they came with warmth, not fear.

Each encounter reminded me that I was not alone, and that the connection between mother and child does not end with distance or death. It endures, unbroken, just waiting to be noticed.

After the experience with the butterfly, I began to spend more time outdoors. I found that being surrounded by nature helped me feel closer to her. I would listen to the sound of the wind through the trees, the rustle of leaves, the buzz of bees. Every sound seemed to carry a message if I was quiet enough to hear it.

One evening, as the sun was setting and the sky was painted in gold and pink, I saw another butterfly drifting through the air. It moved slowly, as if gliding through water, catching the last light of day. I followed it with my eyes until it disappeared into the horizon.

At that moment, I whispered a prayer of thanks.

For my mother, for the peace I had found, and for the reminder that the spirit world does not exist somewhere far away. It moves through the same air we breathe, present in the small, beautiful things that so often go unnoticed.

The butterfly became my symbol of that truth.

To this day, whenever I see one, I still stop and smile. It is my mother's way of saying that love never dies. It only changes wings.

Chapter Eight
The Jesus and the Devil Image

Location: Lakeland, Florida

Time: Good Friday, Early 2000's

For years I had worked as a meteorologist, sending weather reports across the country and studying the way nature balanced itself through storms and sunlight. My instruments could measure air pressure, temperature, and wind speed, but there are forces that no equipment can detect. By this time, I had already experienced the strange presence in my house, heard laughter from nowhere on New Year's Eve, and watched lights flicker in empty rooms. I had begun to accept that the world held more than science could explain.

Still, nothing prepared me for what I was about to witness.

It happened on a quiet Good Friday, one of those clear spring days that carry a stillness so complete it feels sacred. My roommate had once again gone to Mexico to visit his family, leaving the house silent. I had the day off from work and was feeling reflective, thinking about life, faith, and all the unexplained things I had seen.

In one of the closets upstairs, I kept a pair of twenty-inch cymbals from my years playing in various drum and bugle corps. I had played percussion most of my life, first as a teenager and later with groups around the country. Music had always been my second love after weather. But as the years passed, the cymbals became too heavy for my hands, and I had switched to playing baritone horn instead. The cymbals had sat untouched for four years, their brass surfaces darkened with time.

That morning, I felt a sudden urge to take them out. I do not know what brought it on, only that I woke with the thought that I should clean them. Maybe it was the sunshine streaming through the window, or maybe something deeper was nudging me. I went upstairs, opened the closet, and lifted the old carrying case onto the bed.

When I unzipped the case, the smell of aged leather and brass filled the room. The cymbals lay inside, dull with dust.

I took one out and held it toward the window to see how much polish I would need. That was when I saw it.

An image, faint but unmistakable, was on the surface.

I blinked and leaned closer. The shape was not random. It looked like a face, calm and solemn, with eyes, a nose, and a beard. My first thought was that it was a stain or reflection, but as I turned the cymbal in the light, the image remained steady. It was not an illusion of shadow or polish marks. It was etched into the metal itself.

I adjusted my glasses and stared. My breath caught in my throat. The face resembled every depiction I had ever seen of Jesus Christ.

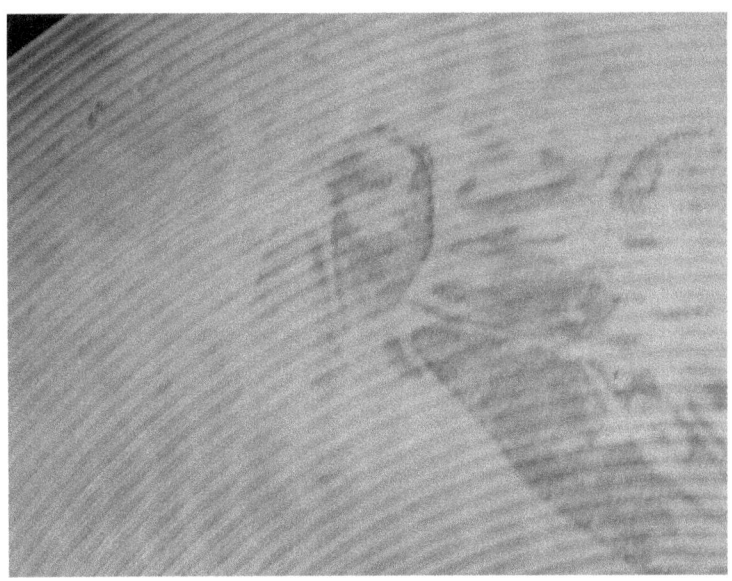

I stood there in stunned silence. For several minutes I could not move. Then, almost in disbelief, I said aloud, "This cannot be real."

But it was.

I ran my fingers gently over the metal. It was smooth, no indentation, no unevenness. The image was not something that could have been drawn or pressed onto the surface. It was simply there.

Then, as if to underline the significance, a realization came over me.

It was Good Friday.

The weight of that recognition filled me with emotion. I had been struggling with my faith in those years. After all the unexplained events in my home, I had begun to wonder if there was a battle of some kind between the light and the dark. Seeing that image on the cymbal felt like a message, a sign meant for me alone.

I decided to take a picture. I placed the cymbal on the bedspread, adjusted the curtains so the light fell evenly, and picked up my digital camera. Looking through the lens, I could clearly see the face of Jesus, serene and detailed. I pressed the button.

The image appeared on the screen, but what I saw made me drop the camera.

It was not the same face I had seen with my eyes.

The photograph showed something distorted, darker, almost grotesque. The eyes were not gentle but sharp. The mouth was twisted into something like a sneer. It was the face of what looked like a demon.

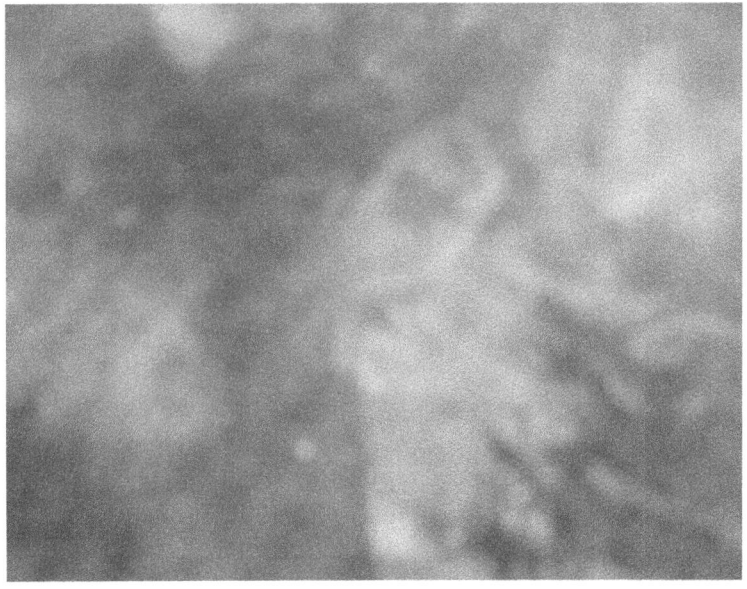

I gasped. My hands shook as I picked up the camera again. I took another photo. Same result. I took a third, then a fourth. Each time, I looked through the lens and saw Jesus, but when the image appeared on the screen, it showed the other face instead.

It was as if something unseen was stepping between me and the truth.

I took one more photo, my heart pounding, whispering a prayer as I pressed the button. When the screen lit up, the image that appeared was once again the calm, holy face of Jesus Christ.

I sank into the chair by the bed, overcome by emotion. There was no other explanation that made sense. I was witnessing a spiritual struggle, a moment of good and evil wrestling over a symbol of sound and faith.

I zoomed in on the pictures, comparing them one by one. The differences were stark. In one image, the expression was kind and peaceful. In the next, the features twisted into something mocking and cruel. When I looked closely, I noticed something else, a small shape near the neck of the image of Jesus. It looked like a bird or perhaps a lizard, its beak or mouth open as if ready to bite.

The detail was too precise to be coincidence. The eye of the creature was visible, sharp and intent. To me, it symbolized the constant struggle between creation and destruction, between the sacred and the profane.

The moment was overwhelming. My hands trembled as I whispered a prayer. "Lord, if this is Your sign, I am listening."

I sat there for hours studying the photos. Each one seemed to hold a different energy. The ones showing the image of Jesus radiated warmth, as though light glowed from the screen itself. The others carried a chill, a heaviness that made me uneasy.

Later that afternoon, I tried polishing the cymbal, thinking perhaps the marks would fade, but they did not. No matter what cleaner I used, the image remained clear and untouched. It was as though the metal itself refused to release what had been placed upon it.

The thought that this could be divine intervention crossed my mind again and again. I remembered how I had felt distant from my faith in those months, how I had questioned whether God still listened. That day, on Good Friday, I received my answer.

The contrast between the two faces reminded me of something deeper than mere vision. It showed me that light and darkness can exist side by side, that even in the same space, one can try to obscure the other, but in the end, truth shines through. The final image, the one that captured the calm face of Christ, was proof to me that the divine always prevails.

That night I could not sleep. I left the cymbals on the bed where I had found the image, too afraid and too awed to put them away. Each time I glanced at them, the image seemed to change slightly depending on how the light struck the metal. Sometimes it appeared clearer, other times faint, but always there.

I thought about how strange it was that an object meant for sound, something that produces vibration and resonance, could become a canvas for something so silent yet powerful. Perhaps the energy from years of music, from parades and performances, had somehow stored spiritual echoes within the metal. Or perhaps, on that holy day, something from beyond had chosen it as a vessel for a message.

The next morning, I went outside and took the cymbal into the sunlight. The image was even more visible under the natural light. It glowed faintly, the outlines sharp, the expression serene. The other cymbal, its twin, remained blank. That was another thing I could not explain. If it had been a trick of oxidation or polish, both would have been marked. Yet only one carried the image.

Over the next several days, I showed the photos to a few close friends. Some were stunned, others skeptical. A few suggested reflections or chemical reactions. But no one could explain why the face changed from photo to photo, why one image showed peace while another revealed darkness.

As time passed, I came to accept it not as a puzzle to be solved but as a revelation to be honored. I did not seek attention or try to make others believe. It was enough that I had seen it, that I knew it was real.

Weeks later, I decided to take the cymbals out again, just to see if the image had changed. I cleaned them carefully, using a soft cloth, yet the image did not fade. It stayed fixed, untouched by time or polish. I placed them back into the case with reverence, as though returning a sacred relic to its resting place.

Every Good Friday since then, I have thought about that day. It reminded me that signs do not always come in grand gestures. Sometimes they appear quietly, on something ordinary, waiting to be recognized.

That day in Florida marked the moment my faith returned to me completely. I no longer doubted whether the divine listened. I no longer wondered if light could still reach me through the confusion of the unknown. The face that appeared on that cymbal was not just an image. It was a reminder.

It told me that God was still near.

Chapter Nine

Vanilla Cupcakes and Spirit Communication

Location: Lakeland, Florida

Time: Early 2000s

Florida has a way of slowing time. Days move more gently here, marked not by deadlines but by sunlight. The air is thick with warmth, the kind that carries the scent of grass and rain. I had been living in Lakeland for several months, long enough for the rhythm of the place to seep into me. The city was quiet, peaceful, and full of small, comforting routines that made me feel at home.

After years of long workdays and constant travel, I finally had the chance to enjoy simple things again. I would wake before dawn to prepare weather reports for my clients, send forecasts to radio stations, and then spend my afternoons tending the garden or reading on the porch. The evenings belonged to the hum of crickets and the deep, calming stillness that seemed to settle over everything once the sun went down.

It was during one of those quiet stretches that I began to notice my mother's presence again.

She had been gone for some time, but her memory was never far. Since the day of the butterfly in the garden, I had learned to recognize the subtle ways she reached out. A song on the radio that played at just the right moment. A sudden warmth that filled the room. A gentle fragrance that reminded me of her perfume. Each time, it felt like a whisper saying, "I'm still here."

One morning, I woke early with a restless feeling. I could not focus on my work, so I decided to spend the day in the kitchen. Cooking had always relaxed me, and baking, in particular, reminded me of my mother. She had taught me how to make simple treats when I was young, teaching me that recipes were not just about precision but about care.

That morning, I decided to make cupcakes.

The kitchen filled with the sounds of small clatters and stirring bowls. I pulled out flour, sugar, butter, and eggs. As I worked, I thought about how much my mother had loved baking. She would hum softly as she mixed batter, her voice blending with the sound of the spoon scraping the bowl.

When it came time to add flavor, I reached for the bottle of vanilla extract. I hesitated for a moment, then smiled and poured in more than the recipe called for. I could almost hear her teasing voice saying, "A little extra never hurts, Tim."

The scent of vanilla filled the kitchen. It was sweet and comforting, wrapping around me like a memory. I put the tray in the oven and waited as the cupcakes rose, golden and fragrant. When they were done, I placed them on the counter to cool, the air rich with warmth and the smell of home.

That afternoon, the house was quiet again. I had nothing urgent to do, so I sat at my desk, sipping coffee, thinking about my mother and the life I was building in Florida. The peace I felt was deep but tinged with longing. I missed hearing her voice. I missed being able to tell her about the strange but comforting experiences that had become part of my life.

After a while, I decided to call a psychic I had spoken to once before. She lived nearly a thousand miles away, but I trusted her. She had been the one who told me about the butterfly in the garden, the one who had said, without me mentioning it, "That was your mother."

When she answered, her tone was calm and kind. "Tim," she said, "how have you been?"

We spoke for a few minutes about ordinary things. I told her I was settling well into Florida, that the air here felt healing, that I was learning to live more quietly. Then I began asking questions about the things I could not explain.

She listened carefully, and then she grew quiet. I could hear her breathing softly, as if concentrating. After a pause, she said, "I smell vanilla."

I froze. "What did you say?"

"Vanilla," she repeated. "Were you baking with vanilla today?"

The words hit me like a wave. My heart pounded. "Oh my God," I said quietly. "Yes, I was. I made cupcakes this morning."

She smiled through the phone. I could hear it in her voice. "Your mother was with you," she said. "She loves that you were thinking of her. She wanted you to know she was right there beside you."

For a long moment, I could not speak. My throat tightened, and tears welled up. The idea that she had been there, right beside me as I stirred the batter and poured the vanilla, was both humbling and comforting.

I finally whispered, "Thank you."

The psychic replied softly, "She wants you to know that every time you think of her with love, she feels it. And when you cook, when you bake, when you fill your home with warmth, that is when she comes closest."

After we ended the call, I sat at my desk for a long time, staring out the window. The afternoon sun streamed through the curtains, painting the room with gold. The scent of vanilla still lingered faintly in the air.

I thought about how much my mother had loved the small, everyday joys of life, a clean kitchen, a blooming garden, the laughter of family. It made sense that she would find her way back to me in those same simple moments.

From that day on, every time I baked something, I felt her near. The sound of the mixer became her humming. The soft smell of vanilla became her presence.

Over the next few weeks, the signs continued. I would catch faint whiffs of vanilla at random times, walking through the garden, sitting in the living room, or even during my morning forecasts. Sometimes it was so strong it made me stop what I was doing. And always, it brought with it the same warmth, the same quiet sense of love.

I began to realize that the boundary between this world and the next is not as firm as we think. Love can cross it easily. It does not need words or hands or even sight. It moves in scent, in memory, in small gestures that speak louder than sound.

That lesson stayed with me. It changed how I saw everything. I no longer needed proof in the form of lights flickering or voices calling. I had come to understand that the spiritual world communicates through feeling. It does not frighten or demand. It comforts.

The day after my call with the psychic, I decided to share what had happened with a close friend from my weather circle. He listened quietly as I spoke. When I finished, he nodded and said, "Tim, maybe faith works the same way as the weather. You cannot see the wind, but you can feel it move through you."

His words made perfect sense.

As a meteorologist, I had spent my life studying invisible forces, currents of air, shifts of temperature, pressure systems that stretched for miles. I could measure their effects but never see the forces themselves. The spirit world, I realized, was much the same. We cannot see it, but we can feel its movement, gentle but powerful, shaping our lives in ways we might never understand.

That afternoon, I went outside with one of the cupcakes and placed it on a small plate in the garden. The air was warm and still. I sat in the grass and whispered, "This one's for you, Mom."

A small butterfly appeared, fluttering near the plate before it flew off into the sunlight.

I smiled. It was enough.

Every time I look back on that day, I think of how ordinary it began. A morning in the kitchen. A batch of cupcakes. A phone call. And yet, it became one of the clearest proofs to me that love is eternal.

When I bake now, I always use a little extra vanilla. Not for flavor, but as a quiet invitation, a way of saying that the door is open, that her presence is welcome. And without fail, I always feel her nearby.

That was the gift Florida gave me, not fear, not mystery, but connection. California had taught me that the unseen exists. Florida taught me that it loves.

The scent of vanilla has never left me. It lingers in the corners of my home, faint but constant, a reminder that my mother is never far away. And whenever I smell it, I stop what I am doing, close my eyes, and whisper, "Thank you, Mom. I still feel you."

Chapter Ten
Dream of the Boss

Location: Lakeland, Florida

Time: Early 2000s

Dreams have always fascinated me. As a meteorologist, I have spent a lifetime studying patterns, the way clouds form, how winds shift, how pressure systems build and fade. Dreams, in their own way, are another kind of pattern. They are currents that rise from places unseen, carrying fragments of memory, feeling, and sometimes, something more.

I had been living in Florida for a few years when the dreams began. Life had settled into a steady rhythm. My mornings were filled with weather reports and calls from radio stations. My afternoons were quiet, often spent in the garden or reading. Nights were peaceful. The strange, unsettling experiences that had once filled my home in

California seemed far behind me. The presence I felt now was softer, like the warmth of sunlight after rain.

Then, one night, I dreamed of someone I had not thought about in years.

In the dream, I was standing inside a newsroom, the kind filled with papers, microphones, and glowing monitors. The air was cool, and I could hear the faint hum of electrical equipment. Across the room, a familiar figure appeared. It was Mike L., my old boss from my years in San Diego.

He looked just as I remembered, confident, smiling, his hair perfectly in place, a cup of coffee in his hand. I felt a rush of nostalgia and warmth. We talked as though no time had passed. He asked how I was doing, if I was still forecasting, and how life was treating me in Florida. His voice sounded exactly the same, calm and good-humored.

When I woke, I smiled to myself. It was nice to see him again, even if only in a dream.

But then it happened again.

The next night, and the night after that, I dreamed of Mike. In each dream, the setting changed, sometimes we were in the newsroom, other times outside under an open sky, but his presence was always the same. He seemed happy to see me, though his tone grew more serious each time. In the third dream, he looked at me and said softly, "Take care of yourself, Tim."

When I woke that morning, I could not shake the feeling that the dream meant something. It was too vivid to be ordinary. There was something in the way he spoke, something final.

For several days, I carried that feeling with me. It was as though the dream had left a trace of energy behind, the same kind I had felt in moments of spiritual connection before. I told myself I was overthinking it. Maybe it was just memory. But deep down, I knew better.

Finally, one afternoon, I decided to act on the feeling. I found the old phone number of Mike's parents, who lived in Arizona. I had not spoken to them in many years, but I felt an urgency I could not explain. I picked up the phone and dialed.

After a few rings, a man answered. His voice sounded familiar but older.

"Hello?"

"Hi," I said, hesitating. "My name is Tim Root. I used to work for Mike in California. Is he around?"

There was a long pause on the other end of the line. Then the man asked quietly, "Who did you say you were?"

"Tim Root," I repeated. "I worked with him in San Diego. I just wanted to say hello."

The man's tone changed, heavy and sad. "Tim," he said softly, "Mike passed away a few days ago."

For a moment, the world went still.

"What?" I asked, my voice barely a whisper.

"He had a heart attack," the man said. "It happened in the shower. We're all still in shock."

I sat in silence, the phone pressed to my ear, my heart pounding. I could hear the faint sound of grief in his voice, the weight of disbelief that comes when loss is still fresh. I offered my condolences and ended the call as gently as I could.

When I hung up, I sat there for a long time, staring at the wall. The dreams replayed in my mind one by one. His face, his voice, the way he had said, "Take care of yourself." It was all so clear now.

He had come to say goodbye.

I felt a rush of emotion, a mix of sadness and wonder. The rational part of me tried to find an explanation. Perhaps my subconscious had picked up on something, a thought, a memory, a sense that time was moving on. But another part of me, the part that had seen lights turn themselves on and off, that had heard laughter from the other side, that had smelled vanilla in an empty room, knew exactly what it was.

It was a visit.

That night, as I lay in bed, I thought about Mike. He had been a mentor to me during my time in California, someone who believed in my talent when I was still finding my voice on the air. He had a way of balancing seriousness with humor, never letting stress show. I had always admired that. It comforted me to think that he had found a way to reach out, even from beyond.

Over the next few nights, I dreamed of him once more. This time, he stood farther away, smiling but silent. Behind him, the sky glowed in soft shades of blue and white. I felt peace in that dream, the kind that comes when something unresolved finally settles. When I woke, the feeling lingered, gentle and light.

That experience deepened my understanding of how the spirit world works. The dead do not always speak through signs or objects. Sometimes, they speak through dreams because dreams are the closest space to their world. It is where the soul can travel freely, unbound by time or distance.

Since that day, I have never doubted the importance of dreams. They are not random. They are bridges.

I began to notice how often people I knew spoke of dreams that carried meaning. Friends told me of loved ones who appeared in their sleep just before or after passing away. Each story carried the same pattern, warmth, light, a message of love, and the unmistakable feeling of farewell.

I thought about how, as humans, we often separate the spiritual from the scientific, believing that one excludes the other. But my life had already shown me that they coexist. Just as invisible air currents shape the weather, unseen spiritual forces move quietly through our lives. You cannot see them, but you can feel their effects.

That understanding gave me comfort. It meant that the world was not divided between life and death, but rather connected by threads of energy and love.

After the dreams about Mike, I began writing down my experiences more carefully. I wanted to keep a record, not just for myself, but for others who might someday read my story and realize that what they felt in their own hearts was real.

There are no coincidences in moments like these. Everything aligns with purpose, even if we cannot see it right away.

A few months later, while organizing some old papers from my years in California, I came across a note from Mike. It was a short thank-you card he had written after a particularly busy week at the station. In his handwriting were the words, "Appreciate all you do, Tim. Keep following the weather, you have a gift for it."

I smiled as I read it. It felt as though he had left me one more message to find, years after his passing.

Sometimes, late at night, I still think about those dreams. I picture him standing there, smiling, surrounded by light, no longer burdened by the worries of this world. And every time I recall his words, "Take care of yourself," I feel gratitude rather than grief.

Because now I understand that when those we love leave this world, they do not vanish. They continue to care, to guide, and to visit in the only ways they can. Through memories, through moments, and sometimes, through dreams.

Chapter Eleven

Bruce's Story

Location: Florida

Time: Mid-2000s

One of the greatest lessons I have learned through all my experiences is that messages from the other side rarely come when you expect them. They appear in moments that seem ordinary, in the quiet, in the pauses, in the details of a day that would otherwise go unnoticed. And they often come when you are least prepared but most in need.

By the time this next story unfolded, I had been living in Florida for several years. I had settled into a calm rhythm. My connection with my mother's spirit through the butterflies and the scent of vanilla had become part of my life, something that comforted me rather than startled me. I had also reconnected with old friends and found new ones through my work in music.

After years of playing percussion in various drum and bugle corps, I joined a local group called the Florida Brass Alumni Drum and Bugle Corps. Music had always been a source of joy and grounding for me. It kept me connected to others and reminded me that energy, whether through sound or spirit, is what binds everything together.

That is how I met Bruce, a good friend and a fellow musician. He played the contra bass horn, a large instrument with a deep, resonant tone that could fill a field with its sound. Bruce was a kind man, practical and funny, the sort of person who could lift the mood of an entire room. We quickly became close friends, sharing not just a love of music but also a sense of curiosity about life beyond what we could see.

Bruce was not a believer in the supernatural. He respected my experiences but often smiled when I spoke of spirits or signs. "You always find the wonder in things," he would say, half teasing, half admiring. I would smile back and tell him, "You will understand one day, Bruce. The signs always find us when we are ready."

That day came sooner than either of us expected.

One morning, Bruce received terrible news. His daughter, who lived in Kentucky, had passed away unexpectedly. The grief that followed was heavy and raw. I could hear it in his voice when he told me. His usual calm and humor were gone. In their place was disbelief and heartbreak.

He traveled to Kentucky to arrange her funeral and settle her affairs. Before he left, I told him quietly, "Bruce, she will find a way to let you know she's still with you. Keep your eyes open, even for the smallest thing."

He nodded but did not answer. I knew he was not ready to believe that yet.

A few days later, I received a call from him. His voice sounded different, softer, as if something inside him had shifted.

"Tim," he said, "you're not going to believe this."

He told me that after the funeral, he had gone to his daughter's house to collect her belongings and take care of final details. It was a two-story home with a staircase that curved gently upward from the living room. Built into the wall along the stairs was a bookshelf filled with her favorite books.

As Bruce walked slowly up the steps, lost in thought, something happened.

A single book fell from the shelf. It landed near his feet, open.

At first, he thought it was a coincidence, perhaps the shelf was loose, or the vibration from his steps had knocked it loose. But when he looked down, he froze. The book that had fallen was her favorite book, the one she had read over and over again, the one she had often told him she loved.

He picked it up and stared at it, unable to speak. The book had not fallen from the edge of the shelf. It had been tucked between others, tight and secure. There was no reason for it to move.

He told me, "Tim, it felt like she was standing right there with me."

He said he sat down on the stairs, holding the book in his hands, and for the first time since her passing, he cried. Not from grief alone, but from a sense of comfort. In that moment, he realized she was still near him.

When he finished telling me, there was a pause on the line. I could hear him take a deep breath.

"I didn't believe in that stuff before," he said quietly. "But now I know she's here."

I smiled, even through the ache in my heart for his loss. "I told you, Bruce. Love always finds a way to speak."

That story became one of the most powerful affirmations I have ever witnessed. Bruce had been a skeptic, a man of logic, but the universe had shown him what words never could. His daughter had found a way to reach out, not through dreams or visions, but through something simple and unmistakable, a falling book that carried her memory and her love.

When he returned to Florida, Bruce seemed lighter. The sadness was still there, of course, but there was peace behind it. He told everyone in the band what had happened. Some listened with curiosity, others with quiet awe. "You can believe what you want," he said to them, "but I know what I felt."

After that, he began to look at the world a little differently. Sometimes, during rehearsal breaks, he would glance at me with a grin and say, "Still think your spirits are the only ones talking?" I would laugh and answer, "You're part of the club now."

Over time, I noticed small changes in him. He spoke about his daughter often, not in sadness but in appreciation. He said he sometimes felt her near when he played, especially during the quiet moments before a performance. "It's like she's listening," he said. "Maybe keeping me in rhythm."

I believed him completely.

Stories like Bruce's remind me that spiritual experiences are not reserved for a few. They happen to everyone, though not everyone notices them. They can come as voices, as dreams, or as gentle movements that catch our attention just long enough to make us stop and think.

For Bruce, it was a book. For me, it had been a light, a butterfly, a scent, a sound. The form does not matter. The message is always the same, love never ends.

A few months after his experience, Bruce told me something else. He had been driving home from rehearsal one night, thinking about his daughter, when a song began to play on the radio. It was a song she had loved, one that always made her laugh when she was younger. The timing could not have been more perfect. "I turned up the volume," he said, "and it felt like she was in the car with me."

He told me that since then, he no longer feared silence. He found comfort in it, knowing it was the space where connection happens.

When I think of Bruce's story, I am reminded that each person's relationship with the spirit world is unique. It does not depend on belief but on openness. You do not have to ask for a sign. You only have to be willing to see it when it comes.

His experience also reinforced something I had felt for years, that spirits find ways to communicate through familiar things. For my mother, it was a butterfly and the scent of vanilla. For Bruce, it was a book. For someone else, it might be a song, a photograph, a flickering light. The form is personal, chosen with love, so we will recognize it.

After his story, I began to share my own experiences more freely. I realized that when we speak openly about the spiritual world, it gives others permission to do the same. People who had kept silent about their own encounters began to tell me what they had seen or felt. There was always hesitation at first, then relief. "I thought I was the only one," they would say.

I would smile and tell them, "You are never alone in these things. The other side is always listening."

Bruce and I continued to play together in the Florida Brass for several more years. Each time we performed, there was a moment when our eyes would meet, and he would nod slightly, as if to say, "She's here." I would nod back, knowing exactly what he meant.

Sometimes, after a particularly moving performance, Bruce would look toward the sky and smile. I never asked what he was thinking. I already knew.

His story stayed with me because it was proof that even the strongest skeptic can become a believer when love reaches across that invisible line. It reminded me that we are all connected, not just by the lives we share, but by the energy that continues after us.

And though Bruce's daughter was gone from this world, she had found a way to let her father know that she was safe, at peace, and still with him.

That is what love does. It endures. It speaks in ways we do not expect. It moves books from shelves, plays songs on the radio, and carries the scent of vanilla through a quiet room.

It is the language of the soul, and it never fades.

Chapter Twelve

An Old Woman and Hurricane Rita

Location: Lakeland, Florida

Time: August 2005

By 2005 Florida already felt like home to me. I had spent several years living in my quiet house in Lakeland, working early mornings on weather reports and enjoying the peaceful rhythm that the state had given me. Hurricane season was in full swing that year, and my days were filled with charts, satellite images, and updates moving across the Gulf and the Atlantic. Even so, nothing about that season prepared me for what happened one August morning. It became one of the clearest messages I had ever received from the spirit world.

That night I went to bed early, tired after a long day of weather monitoring. The house was silent except for the steady hum of the air conditioner. I fell into a deep sleep, the kind that settles over you like a warm blanket. Everything felt still and ordinary.

Then, at around four in the morning, I woke suddenly.

I opened my eyes, expecting to see the soft shadows of my bedroom. Instead, in the far corner, stood the figure of an old woman. Her presence felt solid and real, yet she did not speak with her voice. Instead, I heard her clearly in my mind, calm but insistent.

"There is going to be another hurricane. It will hit Texas in the next couple of weeks. The name will be Rita."

Her eyes stayed fixed on mine. The message repeated silently, word for word, with a certainty that filled the entire room. And then, just as suddenly as she had appeared, she vanished, dissolving into the stillness around me.

I sat up immediately, wide awake. My heart pounded, but it was not fear. It was the clarity of what I had just been told. I got out of bed and walked straight to my weather office on the other side of the house.

I turned on my computer, pulled up the list of hurricane names for the 2005 season, and scrolled down. When I saw the next name on the list, I felt a cold shiver run through me.

Rita.

The old woman's message had been exact. I stared at the screen for a long moment, trying to understand what had just happened.

Over the following days I watched the tropics more closely than ever. A tropical low had begun forming far out in the Caribbean. At first it looked weak, barely enough to draw attention, but something in my intuition made me track it carefully. Each morning it grew more organized as it moved slowly toward the Gulf of Mexico.

Within a week the system strengthened enough to be named. The advisory flashed across the screen.

Hurricane Rita.

I felt a rush of emotion, a mix of shock and recognition. Everything the old woman had told me was unfolding exactly as she had described.

Rita intensified rapidly. The storm grew into a powerful hurricane, spinning with winds near one hundred fifteen miles per hour. The models tracked it steadily toward Texas. The news stations began their warnings. The Gulf Coast prepared for impact.

Two days later, Rita made landfall.

The destruction was immediate. Flooding swept through towns. Winds tore roofs from buildings. Power outages covered entire regions. The storm left a trail of chaos across Texas, just as the woman had said.

That evening I sat quietly, absorbing everything I had witnessed. I watched the news coverage, the reporters speaking over images of broken streets and rising waters, and I thought about the old woman who had stood in my room that morning. Her message had not been dramatic. It had been calm, clear, and purposeful.

She came because I was listening.

In all my years of spiritual encounters, I have learned that messages from beyond arrive when they need to, not when we expect them. They come through voices, through feelings, through dreams, and sometimes, as in this case, through a presence so real you cannot doubt what you have seen.

The woman's message was not meant to frighten. It was meant to prepare. It showed me once again that the spirit world does not live far away. It stands close, watching over us, guiding us when something important is about to unfold.

Rita became one of the most unforgettable hurricanes of that year, but for me it also became something more. It became proof that spirits will speak when they feel we are ready to hear them. And that morning in 2005, at four o'clock in the quiet stillness of my bedroom, an old woman stepped forward to deliver a message I will never forget.

Chapter Thirteen
The Witch's Curse
(Steve's Story, Connecticut)

Location: Monroe, Connecticut

Time: Late 1990s

I have often said that encounters with the spirit world are not confined to one place or time. They follow us, reveal themselves in unexpected ways, and sometimes reach out to others who are not even seeking them. This next story is not my own, but it was told to me by a close friend, and it left a lasting impression.

My friend Steve was a construction worker from Stratford, Connecticut. He was a straightforward man, practical, good at his job, and not easily shaken. Unlike me, he had no deep interest in the paranormal. To him, stories about ghosts and curses were the kind of tales people shared around a campfire, interesting but distant from real life. That changed one morning in the small town of Monroe, Connecticut.

Steve had been hired with his crew to repave a road that ran alongside a very old cemetery, one that dated back to the 1600s. The gravestones were weathered and uneven, their inscriptions faded by centuries of rain and frost. Some of them leaned sideways, half buried in moss, as if time itself had been slowly reclaiming them.

The morning was quiet and cool. The men were waiting to begin work, but the town had a rule that no machinery could start until nine o'clock to avoid disturbing nearby residents. To pass the time, Steve and one of his coworkers decided to take a walk up the hill to explore the cemetery.

They followed a narrow path that wound between the graves. The grass was high and damp, brushing against their boots. Birds called faintly from the trees. Everything felt still, the way old cemeteries often do, as if the air held its breath.

Steve stopped when he noticed one grave that looked newer than the others. The headstone stood tall and clean, its lettering sharp against the gray stone. It read: **Hannah Cranna, wife of Capt. Joseph Hovey.**

He recognized the name immediately. Hannah Cranna was a local legend, known in Connecticut folklore as "the witch of Monroe." People said she had lived in the 1800s and had been feared by her neighbors for her strange behavior and mysterious ways. Some believed she could cast spells, others thought she was simply misunderstood. But the stories always ended the same, after her death in 1859, the people who had mocked her began to suffer misfortunes. Over time, her name became a warning whispered by children and adults alike.

The grave of Hannah Cranna, the Wicked Witch of Monroe, in 2007

Steve looked at the grave with curiosity. On top of the stone were several coins, weathered but gleaming faintly in the light. Locals often left them there out of respect or superstition. Steve, not thinking much of it, reached out and picked up one of the coins. He turned it over in his hand, examining the worn surface. His coworker watched in silence.

After a few seconds, Steve shrugged and placed the coin back exactly where he had found it. "No harm done," he said with a grin.

They started walking back down the hill toward the road. Halfway down, Steve felt suddenly dizzy. The world tilted beneath him, and his legs went weak. He sat down on the grass, breathing heavily. A wave of nausea and lightheadedness swept through him. His coworker ran to his side, alarmed.

Within moments, a police officer who had been patrolling the area noticed them and rushed over. "Are you all right?" the officer asked.

Steve tried to answer but felt his voice catch in his throat. The dizziness grew worse, his skin clammy. The officer called for an ambulance.

At the hospital, doctors ran a series of tests. Heart, blood, balance, oxygen levels, everything came back normal. There was no explanation for his sudden illness. By evening, the dizziness faded, leaving Steve exhausted but unharmed.

When I spoke to him later, he told me, "Tim, it was like something grabbed me. Like the air itself turned against me for a moment."

He believed that what had happened was connected to that coin.

"I think she cursed me," he said quietly. "Hannah Cranna, the witch. They say she guards that grave. Maybe I shouldn't have touched it."

I had heard many ghost stories in my life, but there was something about the calm certainty in his voice that struck me. Steve was not the kind of man to invent things. He had no reason to exaggerate.

For years afterward, he avoided that area entirely. But the story did not end there.

Several years later, Steve's daughter, who shared his growing fascination with the paranormal, asked him to take her to the cemetery where the incident had happened. She wanted to see the grave of the so-called witch for herself.

He hesitated. "I'll take you close," he said, "but I'm not going near that hill again."

They rode their bikes together on a quiet afternoon, following the road that curved through the old neighborhood. When they reached the base of the hill where the cemetery stood, he stopped and pointed. "That's it," he said. "Up there, behind those trees."

His daughter looked up with curiosity, her eyes wide. "Can we go see it?" she asked.

Steve shook his head firmly. "Not me. You can look from here."

They stood for a few minutes, talking softly about the legend, about how stories like Hannah Cranna's survive through generations. Then they decided to continue their ride.

They had barely gone a hundred yards when something unexpected happened.

A car suddenly swerved into their lane, cutting directly in front of Steve. He had to brake hard, his motorcycle skidding on the gravel. For a split second, he thought he was going to crash. The car sped away without stopping, disappearing around the bend. His daughter, who had been behind him, screamed his name, terrified.

When he pulled over to catch his breath, his hands were shaking. He looked back toward the hill, pale and shaken.

"Tim," he told me later, "it was her again. I could feel it. She remembered me."

He was convinced that Hannah Cranna, the witch buried on that hill, had reached out once more to remind him of her warning. The near accident was too precise, too sudden, to feel like coincidence.

I listened quietly as he spoke, letting him tell it in his own words. There was no fear in his tone, only respect. He said, "I don't think she meant to hurt me. I think she just wanted me to remember. Maybe to leave her alone."

It was a story that stayed with me, not because of its drama but because of what it revealed. Steve had not believed in spirits before. He was a man of hard work and simple explanations. But after that day, his view of the world changed.

He no longer dismissed the idea that places can carry energy, that the past can linger in the ground, that actions, even small ones, can awaken something ancient.

When I visited Connecticut years later, I found myself driving through Monroe. Out of curiosity, I took a detour toward the cemetery. The road was quiet, the trees forming a canopy overhead. I parked near the base of the hill and stood for a while, looking upward.

I did not climb the hill. I did not need to. The air itself carried a weight, a silence that was not empty but watchful.

I whispered, "Rest in peace, Hannah."

The wind stirred slightly, rustling the leaves. It could have been coincidence, but I have learned that coincidences are often how the unseen speaks.

Whether you believe in curses or not, I think there are places where emotion becomes part of the land, where sorrow, fear, and memory fuse together, leaving traces that can still be felt centuries later.

Steve's story is a reminder that respect is the key to every encounter, both with the living and the dead. Curiosity is natural, but reverence keeps us safe.

And perhaps, in her own way, Hannah Cranna was never a witch at all, but a woman whose story became legend, whose resting place now watches over those who forget that every soul, no matter how misunderstood, deserves peace.

Chapter Fourteen
Gary's Story

Location: Stratford, Connecticut

Time: 1969

L ong before I ever experienced strange voices, flickering lights, or the presence of the unseen, there was another story in my family that hinted that the spiritual world had always been close to us. It happened many years ago, in 1969, when my brother Gary was a young man.

Gary and I were close growing up. He was adventurous, good-natured, and never afraid of a challenge. He had the kind of confidence that made him seem fearless, whether he was working late nights, traveling, or helping a friend. But there was one night in his youth that left even him silent in awe, a night that became part of the stories we still talk about whenever the subject of the supernatural comes up.

Gary told me this story himself, and I have never forgotten the look on his face as he described it. It took place in a small town not far from an old nineteenth-century cemetery, the kind where the stones lean at odd angles and the air always feels a little cooler than it should.

One summer evening, Gary and a few of his friends planned to spend the night at the home of one of their classmates. The boy's family lived in a large, creaking house that sat directly beside the cemetery. From the upstairs windows, you could see rows of headstones stretching into the distance, their shapes glowing faintly under the moonlight.

The boy's girlfriend was also there, along with Gary and their own dates. They were teenagers then, full of curiosity and laughter, not easily spooked. The boy's mother owned the house, but his father had passed away years earlier. According to the family, the father had been a stern man who strongly disapproved of the relationship his daughter had with her boyfriend. Even in life, he had made it clear that he did not want them together.

As the night fell, the group gathered in the living room, spreading out sleeping bags on the floor. The old house groaned with the sound of settling wood, and every so often the wind carried faint whispers from the cemetery next door. Someone joked about ghosts watching them through the windows, and everyone laughed.

It was around eleven o'clock when the laughter stopped.

They had just started to drift toward sleep when, without warning, a burst of fire shot up from the fireplace. Flames leapt several feet into the air, bright and sudden, lighting the entire room for a few seconds before vanishing as quickly as they had appeared.

The group screamed and jumped back. For a moment, no one moved. The fire had flared violently, yet there had been no heat. When Gary cautiously stepped closer to the hearth, the room was already dark again. The logs inside the fireplace were cold to the touch. There was no smoke, no embers, no lingering warmth. It was as though the fire had never existed.

Gary told me that the air in the room felt heavy after that, as if the house itself were holding its breath. His friends whispered nervously, glancing toward the dark windows that looked out toward the cemetery. Finally, one of them ran upstairs to wake the boy's mother.

When she came down, she seemed calm, almost unsurprised. She listened as they described what had happened, her expression unreadable. Then she nodded slowly and said, "Things like that happen here all the time."

The room fell silent.

Gary remembered how her voice carried no fear, only quiet acceptance, as if she had long since made peace with whatever shared that house with her.

After she went back upstairs, no one could sleep. The faint ticking of a clock sounded like thunder in the stillness. They whispered theories, maybe it was gas, maybe a draft, maybe something electrical, but deep down, everyone knew it was something else.

The next morning, the sun poured through the windows as if trying to erase the memory of the night before. But the marks of the fire, brief as it was, remained in their minds.

When Gary told me this story years later, he said he had never experienced anything like it again. "It wasn't just a trick of the light," he said quietly. "It was real, and it came from nowhere."

I asked him what he thought it meant. He paused, considering. "I think it was a message," he said. "Maybe from the father. Maybe from the cemetery. Someone wanted to be heard."

He believed the fire had been a warning, a way for a spirit to make its presence known, perhaps a protective father's way of saying that the boy in the house was not welcome. Or maybe it was something older, a restless soul from the graveyard next door reacting to the laughter of living voices so close to its resting place.

Whatever it was, Gary said the feeling of being watched had lingered long after the flames vanished.

When I picture that night, I can almost imagine it. The glow of the brief fire reflecting on their faces, the chill that followed, and the uneasy silence that must have filled that room.

It was a haunting without violence, but full of power.

For me, the story carried more than just mystery. It hinted at something I would come to understand deeply years later, that the veil between the physical and the spiritual is thin, and sometimes it flickers open just enough for a message to pass through.

That night in 1969 was long before my own encounters began. At the time, I was still too young to think much of it, but I never forgot Gary's voice when he retold it. It carried that quiet mix of awe and respect that only comes from seeing something you cannot explain.

He said that after that night, he felt different. Cemeteries no longer frightened him, but he approached them with caution. "They're peaceful," he told me, "but not empty."

That line stayed with me. Peaceful, but not empty.

Years later, when my own life became filled with signs from the spirit world, I often thought back to Gary's story. It felt like a kind of foreshadowing, a message that had been sent to our family long before we realized how open we were to the unseen. Maybe the presence that touched my life had first brushed against his. Maybe it was always meant to find us.

Whenever Gary and I spoke about it in later years, his view remained the same. He did not think of it as frightening, but as purposeful. "It wasn't evil," he said. "It was just there. Like it wanted us to know this world isn't the only one."

That perspective shaped how I would later interpret my own experiences. I stopped seeing spirits as intruders and began to see them as messengers, each trying to communicate something, even if we could not always understand the language.

Gary's story stands as a quiet but powerful reminder of that truth.

Even now, decades later, I can picture that moment, the group of friends sitting in the dim light of an old house, laughter turning to shock as fire erupts from nowhere, the strange calm that followed, and the mother's simple words, "Things like that happen all the time."

Those words echo the same lesson I have learned through my own journey, that the world around us is layered with mystery, and sometimes those layers shift just enough for the unseen to show itself.

Whether it was a warning, a sign of protection, or simply an expression of energy from another realm, what happened that night left its mark. And in telling it, Gary passed along a piece of that mystery, connecting his story to mine, like a spark leaping from one fire to another.

It was the first story of spirit I ever heard within our family. The one that came before all the others.

And perhaps it was the world's way of saying that the door between life and death had always been open to us, even back then, in a quiet house beside an old cemetery, where a brief fire burned without heat and a message was sent without words.

Tim Root

Chapter Fifteen
A Whisper From New Hampshire

Location: New Hampshire

Time: Mid 2000s

One quiet weekday afternoon, my thoughts drifted to my dear friend Sharon, who now lives in New Hampshire with her husband, Dan. Their home sits deep in the woods, tucked among tall pines and scattered birch trees. The kind of place where the mornings begin with mist rolling over the ground, and the evenings settle into a peaceful hush broken only by the rustle of wildlife.

Sharon often told me about the deer that wandered right up to their yard, bold enough to look through the windows as if they owned the place. Their cats and dogs would go wild every time a new creature appeared, running from room to room in a frenzy of excitement. It always amused her, and

I could almost hear the laughter in her voice every time she described the chaos.

We had been friends for many years, stretching all the way back to our childhood days in Connecticut. Life had carried us in different directions, as it tends to do, but we never lost our connection. So that afternoon, with her on my mind and the house unusually still, I picked up the phone and dialed her number.

When she answered, the familiar warmth in her voice made me smile. We talked for a while, catching up on the ordinary things—weather, family, pets, memories of the old neighborhood. Then, without warning, a dull ache began to pulse behind my eyes. It was sharp in a strange way, the kind of headache I only ever got when something else was happening, something I had learned not to ignore.

As we talked, a name surfaced in my mind, sudden and clear. Janet. A friend from our Connecticut days. Someone I had not thought about in years. I could almost see her face, as if she had stepped out from some forgotten corner of memory.

So I asked, gently, "How is Janet?"

The reaction on the other end of the line was immediate. Sharon's voice cracked with emotion as she answered, louder than before, "She passed away two weeks ago."

I sat there in stunned silence. I had not heard a thing about Janet's passing. I had no reason to think of her that day. Yet her name had come to me as strongly as if someone had whispered it right into my ear.

In that moment, everything made sense. The sudden headache. The clear push of her name into my thoughts. The urge to ask. I realized Janet had come through to say hello, not to me, but to Sharon. A message delivered the only way I knew how.

You see, I do not call myself a medium. Mediums have a gift far beyond mine. They can speak to spirits, hold conversations, see and hear them with clarity. What I do is different. I channel what comes when it comes. I feel the nudge, the presence, the whisper that isn't a whisper. Sometimes it is for someone close to me. Other times it is for someone who simply needs a message from a loved one who has crossed over.

That afternoon with Sharon reminded me of the strange way these moments arrive. They do not come with warning.

They do not ask permission. They appear quietly, gently, like a soft tap on the shoulder from the other side.

I believe Janet reached out because Sharon needed to know she was still there in some way, watching, remembering, and letting her old friend know she was at peace. It was not dramatic or frightening. It was simple, familiar, and full of warmth. It was Janet's way of saying, "Hi. I'm fine."

And when the moment passed, the headache faded, as it always does. Leaving only the quiet certainty that the connection had been real.

These small encounters are part of my life, woven into my days like threads I never fully control. They do not arrive often, but when they do, I listen. Because every message, no matter how small, is meant for someone. And sometimes, the living need that message more than they realize.

Epilogue
The Other Side of the Storm

Location: Lakeland, Florida

Time: Present Day

When I look back over the course of my life, it feels as though the unseen has always been close. From the first whisper in a dark room to the scent of vanilla in my Florida kitchen, the spirit world has never truly left my side. For years, I tried to separate science from faith, to draw a clear line between what I could measure and what I could only feel. But the longer I have lived, the more I have realized that there is no separation at all. The visible and invisible are not two worlds. They are one, constantly overlapping like layers of weather passing through the same sky.

As a meteorologist, I have always been drawn to patterns. I have spent decades studying the flow of air, the shifting of clouds, and the rhythm of storms. The atmosphere has a voice, one that changes from whisper to roar, yet always speaks with purpose. I have come to believe that the spiritual world is much the same. It moves through us in ways that are quiet but deliberate, touching our lives in moments we least expect.

For me, it began with voices and lights in California. Those first experiences opened my eyes to a reality I could not ignore. The night a young boy's voice called to me, the light that turned on and off by command, the footsteps that echoed on wooden floors when no one was there, they were all part of my awakening. They frightened me at first, but in time I realized they were not warnings. They were invitations.

In El Cajon, I learned that the unseen is not always gentle. It can make its presence known with power, like a thunderclap on a clear day. Yet even then, there was order behind it. Each event seemed connected, each one teaching me something about the balance between fear and faith.

Then came the moments of awe and grace. The image of Jesus that appeared on my cymbal was one of the most profound. That Good Friday will stay with me for the rest of my life. To see His face emerge from metal that had been untouched for years was to witness a miracle. It reminded me that the divine reveals itself through the simplest of things, even through an object meant to create sound.

There were times when darkness tried to interfere. The distorted faces that appeared in my photographs, the shifts between the holy and the unsettling, reminded me that good and evil exist side by side. But in every test, light prevailed. Each time I doubted, faith found its way back.

When I finally left California, I thought perhaps I was leaving those experiences behind. I wanted peace, quiet, and simplicity. Florida gave me that, but it also gave me more. Here, the signs returned not as warnings but as comfort.

The butterfly in the garden that appeared after my mother passed away was one of the most beautiful messages I have ever received. In that single moment, watching its wings catch the sunlight, I felt her love wrap around me as clearly as if she were standing beside me. Later, when the psychic confirmed that the butterfly had been her way of saying hello, I knew it was true.

The scent of vanilla that filled my kitchen when I baked cupcakes was another reminder. My mother had always told me that love never dies, that it changes form but never leaves. Each time the sweet scent drifted through the air, I felt her near, her presence gentle and reassuring. Those moments taught me that the line between heaven and earth is not fixed. It bends for love.

Florida also brought me new lessons through the lives of others. My friend Bruce learned that even those who doubt can be touched by the unseen. His daughter's favorite book falling from the shelf was no coincidence. It was love reaching out, breaking through the silence to say, "I'm still here." Seeing Bruce find peace in that moment reminded me that the spiritual world is not confined to those who believe in it. It finds its way to everyone, especially in moments of loss.

Steve's story about the grave in Connecticut reminded me of the other side of the unseen, the side that demands respect. Some places hold powerful energy, shaped by centuries of human emotion. What happened to him near Hannah Cranna's grave was not cruelty, but a reminder that every soul, even those misunderstood in life, deserves peace and acknowledgment. Respect for the dead is a universal language, one that crosses every boundary between the living and the spirit world.

And then there was Gary's story, the first in our family. Long before any of my own encounters, my brother saw the veil lift for just a moment in that house beside the old cemetery. A fire that burned without heat, a mother who calmly said, "Things like that happen all the time." I have often thought about that night. Perhaps it was the beginning of something larger, a thread that would later connect to my own experiences. Maybe it was the first spark in a long line of messages that would eventually lead to me.

Each of these stories, whether mine or someone else's, has become part of the same pattern. Together, they form a map of how spirit moves through our lives. They are not random or separate. They are part of a greater design, one that reminds us that nothing truly ends.

There have been moments when people have asked me if I ever wish I had lived an ordinary life, one untouched by these mysteries. I always smile and tell them no. I would not trade these experiences for anything. They have given me understanding, purpose, and peace. They have taught me that the afterlife is not a distant place, but a continuation of the same love that binds us here.

The most important thing I have learned is that faith and awareness go hand in hand. You do not have to seek out the spirit world. You only have to keep your heart open. The signs will find you when you need them. They might come as a voice, a dream, a scent, a flicker of light, or even a memory that suddenly feels alive again. The form does not matter. What matters is the message, that we are not alone, and that love continues beyond the limits of this life.

I often think of my work with weather as a mirror to all of this. The atmosphere is invisible, yet it moves everything. You cannot see wind, but you can see what it does. You cannot see faith, but you can feel its strength when the world feels uncertain. You cannot see love, but it leaves traces everywhere.

Sometimes, when I stand outside at night watching clouds drift across the sky, I feel the same presence I felt all those years ago in that quiet California room when the light turned on by itself. It is a presence that does not speak in words but in feeling. It says, "You are watched over. You are loved."

If these stories have taught me anything, it is that our souls are not bound by distance, time, or form. They move freely, guided by something far greater than we can understand. I have seen proof of that in the laughter of unseen guests on New Year's Eve, in the face of Christ appearing on a cymbal, in the flutter of a butterfly's wings, and in a book that fell to the floor to say, "I am still with you."

Every sign has carried the same truth, that life and death are not opposites, but companions. They exist together, one flowing into the other like night turning into dawn.

The storms of life will always come, and so will the calm that follows. I have learned to see both as gifts. The storms remind us that we are alive. The calm reminds us that we are guided.

Now, as I write these final words, I feel deep gratitude. Gratitude for the life I have lived, for the people I have loved, and for the moments that proved beyond doubt that this world is not the end. There is more waiting for us, something beautiful and endless.

When my time comes, I will go without fear. I have seen enough to know that what lies beyond is not darkness, but light. It is the same light that flickered in my room that first night, the same light that glowed through the wings of a butterfly, the same light that shines in every act of love.

Our souls are weathered by life, just as the earth is weathered by storms, but through every change, one truth remains. Love endures. Faith endures. And somewhere, beyond the clouds, those we have lost are still watching, still guiding, still waiting to welcome us home.

www.ingramcontent.com/pod-product-compliance
Lightning Source LLC
Chambersburg PA
CBHW051214120626
46547CB00013B/1346